Industrial Action

Trade Union Industrial Studies

This series makes two new types of provision in the area of
industrial relations: first it is specifically directed to the needs of
active trade unionists who want to equip themselves to be more
effective, and second, the books are linked together in a series
related to the requirements of existing training and education
courses.

The books have been designed by a Curriculum Development Group
drawn from the Society of Industrial Tutors: Michael Barratt Brown,
Ed Coker, Jim Fyrth, Bob Houlton and Geoffrey Stuttard,
together with Charles Clark and Francis Bennett of the Hutchinson
Publishing Group. The Curriculum Development Group has prepared
the guide lines for the texts and edited them so that they form a
complete set of teaching material for tutors and students primarily
for use on trade union courses.

The texts are issued in sets of four, together with an accompanying
resource book which provides additional background material for
tutors and students.

Trade Union Industrial Studies

This series is published in three sets, each consisting of
four student texts and an accompanying resource book. This
book includes additional teaching material for tutors and
students, a recommended list of books and a further exploration
of the subjects by the authors of the texts.

The Activist's Handbook   *Bob Houlton*
Statistics for Bargainers   *Karl Hedderwick*
Calculating   *Joyce & Bill Hutton*
The Organized Worker   *Tony Topham*
Industrial Studies 1: the key skills   *Eds. Coker &
    Geoffrey Stuttard*

Industrial Action   *Ernie Johnston*
Pay at Work   *Bill Conboy*
Work Study   *Jim Powell*
Workers' Rights   *Paul O'Higgins*
Industrial Studies 2: the bargaining context   *Eds. Ed Coker &
    Geoffrey Stuttard*

The Union Rule Book   *Richard Fletcher*
Opening the Books   *Michael Barratt Brown*
Trade Unions and Government   *Ossie O'Brien*
Industrial Studies 3: understanding industrial society
    Eds. Ed Coker & Geoffrey Stuttard

Ernie Johnston

Industrial Action

Arrow Books
in association with the
Society of Industrial Tutors

Arrow Books Ltd
3 Fitzroy Square, London W1

An imprint of the Hutchinson Publishing Group

London Melbourne Sydney Auckland
Wellington Johannesburg and agencies
throughout the world

First published in 1975
© Ernie Johnston 1975

Made and printed in Great Britain by litho
by The Anchor Press Ltd
Tiptree, Essex

ISBN 0 09 911880 7

Contents

Introduction: a Personal View   7

1 Organizing a New Factory   11

Early Days   11
Taste of Success: the 1964 Strike   12
Setback: the 1966 Lock-Out   13
What Can Be Learnt?   15
The Threat of Action   17

2 The Job of the Strike Committee   18

The Job in Brief   18
Keeping Aims Clear   18
Discipline and Unity   19
Contact with Union Officials   20
Reporting to the Media   21
Transport   21
Delegations   21
Cash   22
The Mass Meeting   23
Administration   24
Blacking   24

3 Close-Range Weapons   25

The Overtime Ban   25
The Miners' Claim and Their Overtime Ban   25
The Overtime Ban Against Unemployment   30
Working to Rule   31

4 Who's in Charge?   33

The Sit-In   33
The Fisher Bendix Sit-In   35
The C.A.V. Sit-In   38
Questions   41

Contents

5 The Militant Works On   43

The Work-In   43
The Upper Clyde Work-In   44
The Triumph Meriden Work-In   47
The Most Important Lessons and Questions   48

6 Picketing   51

Your Rights?   51
Some Basic Hints   52
The Mass Picket   53
Roberts Arundel   53
The Flying Picket   54
Conspiracy   54

7 Some Thorny Problems   57

Disputes Between Unions   57
The Strike Against the Union, Pilkingtons, 1970   58
The Strike Promoted by the Employer   60

8 Action in the Factory and the Combine   63

Levels of Action   63
Action in the Factory   63
Action in the Combine   66
The Ford Combine Committee and the 1971 Wage Claim   67
The Dillon Affair   67
Guerrilla Tactics in the Combine   68
Dunlop Pirelli: the International Strike   70
The Future Role of Combine Committees   71

9 Action in One Industry   73

The Manchester Experiment, 1972   73
The Post Office Strike, 1971   78

10 The Real Face of the Employer   82

Employers' Solidarity   83
Who Keeps Who?   85
The Immediate Task   85

Introduction: a Personal View

When asked to write this book, I asked myself 'Who am I to give others advice?' Then, when I realized that time had passed so quickly that I had forgotten that I had behind me over twenty-three years as an active trade unionist, I thought perhaps that experience alone permitted me to offer others my advice on the problems of industrial action.

A fair part of this book is drawn directly from my own experience. For instance, I lived through as convenor all the happenings at the Lucas C.A.V. site, with the exception of the sit-in. As I had for many years played an active role on my District Committee and was for five years a member of the National Committee of my union, I naturally paid keen attention to what was going on around me in other factories and industries. This interest, along with a reasonably broad experience, gives me at least minimum qualifications which have persuaded me that my advice may be of some value.

No one more than myself realizes that there is a danger that I may have been too subjective. I can only say that I have striven conscientiously to avoid this.

It must not be thought that this book is written just for the militant trade unionist. Even the most moderate of us will find that there are occasions when no matter how patiently we have negotiated, the employer refuses to meet a reasonable claim. The starting point of this book is the assumption that no further progress can be made by negotiation and that some form of action has to be taken. I have attempted to forewarn those who take action, against some of the pitfalls which may await them and to give advice on how to be positive in that action.

Having said that, I should reveal my own views on employers (some call them prejudices). I have been a socialist all my adult life, convinced that we are exploited by the employers. I see no other solution than the continuation of the class war to final victory. It is to assist that aim that this book has been written.

Without in any way pretending that we have no need for a political arm, I maintain that the strongest expression of working-class power, at the moment, is the trade union movement.

The one great danger that I see is the splitting of the working class into different 'pure doctrinal groups'. It may be a sobering thought for them, that in the instances described in this book where victories were won, they were won by a united effort of all the best elements of our class. By best elements I mean all those who are prepared to fight, sometimes against the tide, for the right to organize independent of the employers' wishes. Conversely, when I refer to reactionary elements, I mean those workers who openly oppose any form of action, no matter how justified.

In defeat, if we will critically analyse our defeats and not make slogans out of them, perhaps we will be better armed for the next battle. In this way, even defeats play a valuable part in helping us build up our armoury.

Since I wrote the first text of this book some time has passed and we have seen the Industrial Relations Act relegated to the history books. I have decided not to omit my original references to the Act but merely to change the tense. The simple reason for this is that action taken against trade unionists under the

Conspiracy and Protection of Property Act 1875 flowed naturally from the Industrial Relations Act. Not only is it necessary to show this here, but it is now vital that trade unionists carrying out their legitimate activities should be immune from the 1875 Act.

For those who have just joined the ranks of activists, I should point out that I have used terminology familiar to me as a member of the Amalgamated Union of Engineering Workers, for example, terms like 'shop steward', meaning a shop-floor representative, and 'District Committee', meaning the committee in charge of local policy. The reader should translate these terms into the ones used in his own union.

Finally, this work has been done as part of my studies at Ruskin College where I spent 1972–4. My thanks go to Ed Coker who has striven hard to help me make this book reasonably intelligible. That he may not have been entirely successful is my fault, and not his.

Note

As well as the sources cited at the end of each chapter, I have interviewed miners, post office workers, members of the Fisher Bendix sit-in committee, members of the C.A.V. sit-in committee, members of the Dunlop Pirelli steering committee, members of T.A.S.S. and engineering workers. I have also drawn on many newspaper reports. Finally, I have used my own experience.

1 Organizing a New Factory

Early Days

In May 1961 the Lucas combine started production on their newly bought site at Fazakerley, Liverpool. A few months later, C.A.V., a subsidiary of the Lucas combine, also began production on the same site.

The workers from these factories had a lot in common. They shared the same car park, canteen, wage department, surgery, personnel department, site entrance and low rates of pay.

Through that site entrance poured a new labour force. Among the skilled workers trade unionism was fairly high, but it was almost non-existent among the rest. To win over these neutral workers was the first task of the small shop stewards' committee. Workers were reluctant to join the union until it could be shown that the union could deliver the goods, yet nothing could be delivered until management was faced with a reasonably united work force.

Many workers found their own solution to the low wages: they left. The few workers who had joined the union were gone before you could hand them their union cards. Yet though this situation acted against organization, it also acted against management. High labour turnover equals high scrap figures. Grudgingly management conceded, in part, the stewards' demands for higher wages. The first concession had been won without a shot being fired and the turnover of labour slowed to manageable proportions.

Consolidating

During the next three years the shop stewards, faced with common wage rates and conditions, sensed the need to organize on a site basis. They met as a site committee and elected a site convenor. Divide and rule was management's policy. Never would management agree to a site convenor although the position over one department was difficult, and everyone knew it. This was the department of maintenance workers, who were housed in one block but for the purpose of administration were on the Lucas factory's payroll and serviced both factories. They had always enjoyed the right to call on the Lucas convenor, who was also the unofficial site convenor. Suddenly, in May 1964, the management withdrew his right to enter the maintenance block. Management had hit at the most strongly organized group of workers and without hesitation the maintenance lads walked out.

Taste of Success: the 1964 Strike

In this dispute, management created its own downfall. All too often in the past the statement had been: 'No negotiation until normal working.' Then, when normal working was resumed, nothing was conceded.

The maintenance crew meant business. They would stay out until they had won. The laying off of half the work force still found the strikers solid, and after ten days management conceded to local union officials the maintenance workers' rights to have their convenor available without strings, although he was not formally recognized as site convenor, a key issue which was to cause further trouble. The settlement was reached on a Friday and the officials, at management's request, urged the strikers to work the weekend to allow as many as possible of the laid-off workers to start back on the Monday. Even with this effort it was made clear that not all the workers could be restarted at once.

Suddenly, a striker was demanding to be heard. He said: 'This strike is all management's fault. There should be no return to work until management agrees to restart all the workers en bloc, whether there is work for them or not.' The laid-off workers, who had turned up at the site to get wages due to them, were standing round the edge of the meeting. A spontaneous cheering broke from them. The officials trudged back to management with the new demands. For over an hour nothing happened, and then the officials came back and announced that management had agreed to restart the whole labour force on the following Monday. No one could be heard above the cheers of workers who had tasted their first victory. Who could say now that trade unionism brought no benefits? Was the determination of the strikers used to the best effect? Events were to prove that it was not, but for the moment this went unnoticed among the delighted leaders.

Where Next?

After the 1964 strike there was a definite change on the site. There was no difficulty now in getting most people to join the union, yet the development of union consciousness was uneven. The Lucas workers almost always carried out the advice of their stewards and acted collectively, but in C.A.V. there was a tendency for each section to act in isolation. It became clear that site unity must be built in order to achieve really effective action. Since the 1964 strike management had appeared to tacitly recognize a site convenor. He had two roles: he was site convenor and Lucas convenor. The Lucas stewards won the workers over to evenly spreading piece-work earnings across the factory; merit rates were slowly eroded. Almost all gains were won after direct action, for management resisted all claims until action was taken.

In C.A.V. progress was much slower, with little uniformity in piece-work earnings or the erosion of merit rates. Many hot arguments took place on the site committee. The Lucas stewards argued that the C.A.V. stewards should unify rates and conditions on a general basis in their factory. Slowly, however, small gains were made, again as a result of direct action and with the C.A.V. convenor insisting that the site convenor be in on all major negotiations.

Setback: the 1966 Lock-Out

Any developing organization must encourage the *fullest participation of all classes of workers*. By 1966 the site committee no longer relied on skilled workers as stewards. This, though, brought its own problems, since many of the new stewards were inexperienced, particularly in the C.A.V. factory. They became impatient with the tactical struggle for unified rates and demanded site action to remove the inequality in piece-work earnings. They insisted that unless action was taken at once, there would be a large drop in union membership in C.A.V.

It was decided, after much hesitating, to test the members' reactions at a site meeting. The meeting agreed unanimously to ban piece-work until considerable improvements were made in piece-work allowances. So, in January, the ban began. It all but halted production. On 5 February, the A.U.E.W. District Committee endorsed the members' action. The following Monday all pieceworkers were locked out. Then the District Committee reversed its policy, and instructed the workers to go back and accept the existing piece-work standards, pending the setting up of a working party. The workers now faced a two-pronged attack, and at the four mass meetings which followed, a hostile District Secretary and Divisional Organizer joined management in trying to persuade the workers to return so that the working party could operate.

Then the tactic was changed. An inquiry at the highest level was offered. There would be joint chairmen, one of whom was to be one of our own national officials, and the other a high-ranking member of the Engineering Employers Federation. The inquiry was portrayed by the officials as a means of solving all the ills which had befallen the workers since the site had opened. In spite of warnings from the stewards, the members, impressed that a national official would enquire into their conditions, voted, by a small majority, to return to work.

The Inquiry

The inquiry took place at the site on 16 March. The stewards had forwarded a list of twenty-six anomalies in the piece-work system. To this written evidence they added verbally another eighteen instances of management's abuse of existing agreements.

The management's evidence consisted of little else than an attack on the site convenor. 'He spent all his time on trade union business.' 'He concerned himself with C.A.V. when he had no right to.' 'He had created a situation where neither factory manager could operate effectively because of him.'

The joint chairman made it clear that they could not solve the problems raised by the stewards. However, this was the basis on which a return to work had been obtained. They rejected the need for a site convenor; they instructed him to spend less time on union activities, do more work for the company and confine himself to the affairs of his own factory. So the great committee of inquiry, the cure for all ills, led nowhere but backwards.

The outstanding claim on piece-work conditions was handled at a works conference two weeks later. Neither the District Secretary nor the Divisional Organizer would touch the case. It was left to the Assistant Divisional Organizer to salvage what he could. He extracted another 1s. 4d. (6½p) from management to be added to 6s. 8d. (33p) offered just before the lock-out. Should the matter have been pursued through the procedure? We knew only too well that the case would have been handled at national level by the same national official who, as joint chairman of the inquiry, had done so much to undermine our authority. For our part we accepted the 8s. (40p).

The Sack

After the enquiry the stewards were faced with two problems. The first was how to halt the growing non-unionism arising from the workers' disillusionment and the second was how to get our union to release copies of the inquiry which had been signed by both chairmen as a true record. Despite all our efforts we could not get our Executive Council to agree to issue even our District Committee with copies until it was too late.

In September, the site convenor was faced with a dilemma. A serious issue had broken out in C.A.V. The C.A.V. convenor was on the opposite shift. The C.A.V. stewards gave warning that unless the issue was dealt with, there would be a further loss of union members. The site convenor went into C.A.V. and, two hours later he was sacked for trespass. The management said that it was clearly recorded in the inquiry minutes that under no circumstances would the convenor go into C.A.V. again. Therefore, on the basis of the evidence of a document to which he was denied access, the site convenor was sacked. By now we were aware that the 1964 strike had not been the complete success we had thought it was at the time.

The fight to have him reinstated is a continuation of this story and will be dealt with later.

What Can Be Learnt?

Let us now examine some of the most important points arising from this short history, for there are lessons to be learned. The questions are asked and answered to make sure those lessons are understood.

We can see already from just two strikes the importance of such things as:

1. Effective factory leadership.
2. The support of union officials.

Questions	1964 Strike	1966 Lock-out
1. Was the stewards' leadership effective enough?	*No.* The stewards set their sights too low. They should have fought for and won the issue of site convenor, preventing the fiasco of the convenor's sacking in 1966.	*No.* They failed to realize that the piece-work ban would lead to a lock-out. They did not prepare the workers for this.
2. Was the official leadership effective?	*Yes.* But note that the District Secretary was involved in a re-election ballot.	*No.* It was appalling at all levels with the exception of the Assistant Divisional Organizer who was not allowed to get involved.
3. Was everything done to get more support from officials?	It was not necessary.	*No.* We should have lobbied our Executive with as many workers as possible participating.
4. Was picketing effective?	*Yes.*	*Yes.*
5. Was blacking effective?	*Yes.* Internal blacking by those still working took place.	*Yes.* Pickets ensured nothing went in or out.
6. Was an attempt made to prevent further management threats?	*No.* See answer to question no. 1.	*No.* Whatever his motives, the convenor should not have gone into C.A.V. after the inquiry.
7. Was timing important?	*Yes.* Order books were full.	*Yes.* The C.A.V. order books were reasonable. The Lucas books were low.
8. Was financial support good?	*Yes.* Production Workers levied themselves before lay-off. This was enough for the small amount of workers involved.	*No.* Apart from the C.A.V. factories in Acton the response was poor.
9. Were the right tactics used?	*Yes.* The use of key workers was ideal.	*No.* We slowed production down far too much, ensuring a lock-out. (See pp.31-2)

3. Fighting to get that support.
4. Effective picketing.
5. Effective blacking.
6. Preparing for management reprisals.
7. Timing: *when* you act is as important as *how*.
8. Cash.
9. The use of the correct tactics.

We need, though, to go much further and enlarge our view to take in the whole scene. We should, for example, consider what weapons are available and the different levels at which they are used.

The Threat of Action

This book is for the practitioner. From the start you must bear in mind this one important point: the threat of action is perhaps the most valuable weapon of all, simply because when it is effective it is the most economical. To be successful *always* observe one golden rule: *never bluff*. Once you have been caught out threatening management with action when you know your members will not support you, your whole position will be undermined. The management will have good reason for doubting you in the future, even when you can deliver the goods. This can cause both sides to dig in their heels, which may result in a long weakening strike. The threat of action is only valuable when management knows that you mean what you say.

Let us then go on to consider the major aspects of industrial action. A word of warning: even the most elementary points will be dealt with, so a little patience is needed. We are engaged on serious business and have no right to leave out simple stages on the false assumption that everybody knows.

SOURCES

1. Minutes and letters Lucas C.A.V. Shop Stewards' Committee, 1964–6.
2. Minutes and letters to and from A.U.E.W. Liverpool District Committee, 1964–6.
3. Minutes of Inquiry into Lucas C.A.V. site, 16 March 1966.

2 The Job of the Strike Committee

The Job in Brief

The purpose of a strike committee is to do all it can to win a strike. It will not be effective unless duties are delegated as much as possible. The diagram (see below) shows the main areas a strike committee deals with. Each area will then be looked at in detail.

Keeping Aims Clear

Often during a strike workers will remember old sores which have nothing to do with the strike. As the strike develops they become more bitter and demand that there should be no return until these are dealt with. If you are not careful, you end up with a shopping list of demands not remotely connected with the issue you came

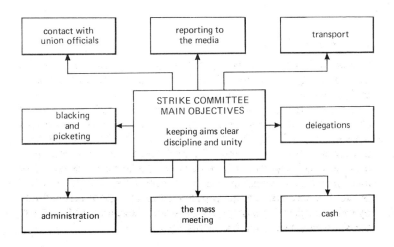

out on. Don't let it happen. The job of the strike committee is to keep to the issue. Impress this on the workers from the start.

If you have won your objectives in spite of scabs, don't let them prevent your return. When you are back at work, toolboxes, work done and even lockers go missing. It sometimes happens in the best-run factory, doesn't it?

Discipline and Unity

Firstly, it is no use impressing how essential these are on the workers if the strike committee itself acts like an undisciplined rabble; but it happens too often.

During normal working, the convenor is used to 'being in charge'. This tendency often flows over into a strike committee with harmful effects. The convenor *must* curb any urge he may have to be a 'one-man band'. People delegated to perform important jobs will not react enthusiastically to being overruled. The convenor is usually responsible for coordinating the different tasks of the strike committee. He should do this by encouragement and by being prepared to accept, for instance, the rulings of the picket marshals when he is on the picket line.

If, despite all efforts, morale suffers or jobs are not getting done because of neglect, then the problems should be raised with the committee at once. Strike committees are no place for dead wood; it *must* be pruned in the interests of the strike.

Contact with Union Officials

You must do all you can to get official support for a strike. It is nonsense to attack officials if they are unaware of your problems. However, it must be admitted that even when they are aware of the problems they sometimes do not provide full support. You must find out why. Don't hesitate to send a strong delegation to either local or national officials, or both. Determined people have a habit of politely but firmly changing the minds of people in high places. If a number of unions are involved, lobby the lot.

If you have to carry on without official support, continue your demands for recognition, but remember you will be accused of unconstitutional action. It's as well to know that officials break the rules when it suits them. For example, the A.U.E.W. Rule Book quite clearly states that 'All correspondence . . . issued in relation to the business of the Union in accordance with rule, by or on behalf of the Executive Council shall bear the imprint of the Executive Council seal.' Yet an extract from the Executive Council Minutes for 7 September 1961 shows that the Executive Council decided that 'the General Secretary [should] send a telegram to R. Birch instructing him to instruct our members to resume normal working'. In the same vein a letter was sent to the Liverpool District Committee with instructions to end a piece-work embargo. The letter had these words on the top: 'Text of letter dictated over telephone 16.2.66'. Neither telegrams nor letters dictated over the phone can possibly bear the seal of the Executive Council. Not only have you a right to ignore such instructions, but you should inform your members of such abuses, which will help them realize that you are not the only ones who break the rules. It will also go a long way towards removing from you the label of demon wreckers.

Apart from workers in struggle there are no greater allies than officials who support you. But there are no worse enemies than those who don't, so watch them. Remember that you will never know if they are acting outside your unions' rules or agreements, if you don't know them yourselves.

So know your Rule Book, your union policy and your agreements.

Reporting to the Media

Winning public opinion can be important, so when reporting to the press and television, it is vital to make one person only responsible for this. Too many views will only cause confusion and contradictions and detract from your case in the eyes of the public. *The Activist's Handbook* by Bob Houlton in this series is very helpful about how to handle the media.

Transport

A strike committee needs to be as mobile as possible. Encourage as many workers as you can to put their cars at your disposal with drivers, if possible.

Just a few words of warning. It is likely these days that the police will be watching you, so make sure that your cars meet all legal requirements; having an M.O.T. certificate is not enough. Cars must be roadworthy; check that they are. Make sure that they are adequately insured and that they are road-taxed. Drive carefully and keep to speed limits. You just can't afford to be picked up.

Try to keep a spare car at the strike headquarters. You never know when you will need it.

Delegations

Make it clear to the workers that delegations are not jaunts for the boys but investments in the strike, intended to raise money or another type of support. Make sure the delegates themselves understand this.

If they are going any distance you may decide that they should visit a number of factories. If this means being away overnight, make sure they phone in daily to report. Nothing is more annoying than delegations wandering the country without anyone knowing what they are up to. Impress on the delegates that they should be factual, cool and disciplined.

Cash

In the last chapter of this book you will see how important the employers consider money is in a strike. They do not think that strikes are industrial regulators or that they help towards quick settlements; for them a strike is war and cash is a vital weapon. I accept the employers' definition. It is war and cash is vital to the winning of it.

For our purposes there are two main problems. One is getting cash, the other is dishing it out.

Getting Cash

In an unofficial strike there are two main sources of cash, donations and Social Security. The first is just hard work. Letters have to be written appealing to every possible organization which might help and speakers have to be sent to as many factories as you can. Don't think you will always be treated fairly on Social Security; you may need help. Sometimes a sympathetic Local Councillor will offer help; accept it. The Claimants Union can also give valuable advice on your rights and you should contact it. Their headquarters address is 19 Rea Tower, Mossborough Crescent, Newtown, Birmingham 19.

In an official strike you may be entitled to more than strike benefit. The A.U.E.W. rules permit a ballot for a district levy. Get your District Committee to ask the Executive Council for permission to hold the ballot.

Dishing Cash Out

You must be scrupulously fair and efficient. Watch carefully every penny spent. Nothing is more demoralizing than the suspicion that something is wrong with the funds. Ensure that the Treasurer's statement is audited at least weekly.

Some workers will have special problems, so you should set up a hardship committee; but take care not to be fooled. If you can, make sure that all cases are vouched for. Remember it's the workers' cash; you're minding it for them.

The Mass Meeting

In one sense the mass meeting is the fulcrum point of the strike. Here decisions are won and lost. It should be a positive weapon, used to build workers' confidence and consciousness. Some simple points will help here.

Avoid pub times for your meetings, since drunken men are seldom given to reason. Always remind your members why you are on strike and what conditions you will return on. Prepare a written reply to any management statement, distribute it at the meeting and go through each of management's points and your answers. Remind your members of all the gains won by the union despite management opposition. Make sure that your strongest supporters mingle with the weak ones, whom you will find often gather in groups. Always put the point that though you are certain that a majority will vote with the strike committee, every vote against raises management's hopes and prolongs the strike. Persuade; don't bully, but don't be bullied. Report on all the activities of the strike committee and then ask all those who are active in the strike to raise their hands. Invite the rest to help. Workers soon gain confidence once they are engaged in activity and never cease to surprise with their audacity. Take a vote at every meeting about carrying on the strike; people resent being taken for granted. Avoid being carried away. Workers will make suggestions which may sound fine in the heat of a meeting, but may result in wild adventures. Ask the meeting to refer all such ideas to the strike committee for deeper consideration.

Simple tactics such as these change a mass meeting and make it a positive weapon for victory.

Administration

The office work required to run a strike is a headache for the committee. It is nearly always the weakest area and unless it is watched, it can lead to a breakdown in communications. Elect an office manager, and make sure he understands that he is responsible for all paper work and that those who work under him should do exactly what he says. This is the only way to maintain order. Remember that when the strike is over you will almost certainly want to keep the records. Apart from anything else, the analysis of your actions after the strike is invaluable knowledge.

Blacking

The motive for strike action is not simply to stop the employer's production; it is also to immobilize as many of his products as possible. To do this, you need strong picket lines. You also need to realize that one of the purposes of delegations is calling on other workers not to handle these products.

Picketing

This issue is so important that a separate chapter has been devoted to it.

SOURCES

1. A.U.E.W. Rule Book.
2. Rootes Dispute: A.U.E.W. Executive Council Minutes, 1961.
3. Claimants Union Handbook.

3 Close-Range Weapons

The Overtime Ban

This is a weapon which needs to be used carefully. As a tactical weapon within a broader strategy it can have great value. As a final weapon with no back-up, its usefulness is less certain, although it may work for less important issues.

Warning! The management does not consist of passive on-lookers. It consists of people who are capable of elaborate pre-parations. In any action, short of coming out on strike workers are far more subject to managerial propaganda than is thought.

A study of two case histories will best illustrate the points made.

The Miners' Claim and Their Overtime Ban

The National Union of Mineworkers is not alone in being unable to call a complete stoppage of its members without a ballot first. But it does have power to call for action falling short of a total strike. This gives it the opportunity to use tactical weapons in the interest of longer-term strategy.

A Paltry Offer, October 1973

Faced with an offer from the Coal Board which was nothing like enough and a Prices and Incomes Policy which seemed to prevent an offer coming anywhere near their claim, the N.U.M. leaders called for a ban on all overtime.

The Effects of the Ban

It is almost certain that if the N.U.M. leaders had called for a strike ballot at this stage, the call would have been rejected by the members; a strike decision had to be fought for. The use of an overtime ban, however, ensured that the industry would be affected. The coal usually cut during overtime hours was no longer available, and the actual output for normal hours fell because

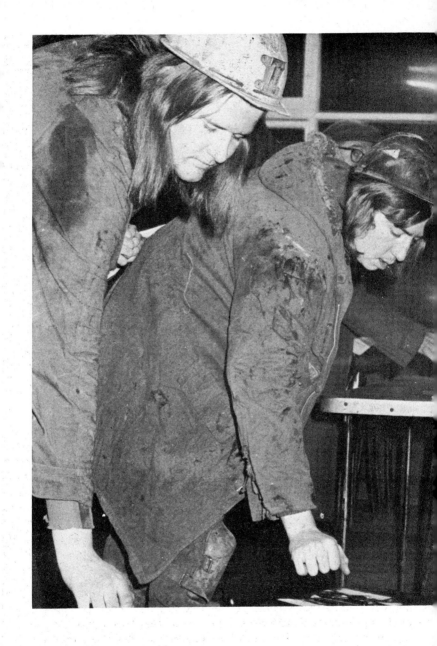

essential maintenance work, which was normally done during weekend overtime, had to be done in ordinary working hours, slowing and sometimes halting production.

The Real Employer

When all the niceties have been removed, few can doubt that the Government is the miners' employer. This employer, with bitter memories of the bloody nose received from the miners in 1972, indulged in the most vicious campaign against the miners. What effect did it have? The miners' reasoning was something like this:

'If after the introduction of an overtime ban manufacturing industries have been reduced to a three-day week, then our work is a lot more important than our wages show. If the three-day week isn't necessary, then we're being used by a crowd of people who are in a mess and need a scapegoat. Besides, they lie like pigs in straw. No matter what the public think, we know that few of us will get anything like the much heralded 16 per cent offer.'

A Moderate Leader

The early stages of the Government's campaign did not divide the miners from their leaders, so the temperature was raised. The miners were presented as the dupes of a handful of extremists, hardworking but foolish men, being used for political ends. One moderate local leader tried to avoid some of the mud sticking to him. His statement undermined the union's stand to win the full claim. His own members, well known for their moderation, demanded and got a retraction from him. Not much of an incident, but a perfect barometer for judging the now stormy mood of the miners.

The Government Manoeuvre

Next, McGahey was singled out for attack. Statements by the militant Vice-President of the N.U.M. were used as proof of his subversive activities. At the same time the Government announced that the three-day week might be relaxed. Whatever the public thought, the miners were unimpressed. They had seen their leaders abused, the offer made completely distorted, and the T.U.C.'s assurance that no other union would quote the miners' case in their own claim, dismissed out of hand. All they had to look forward to were promises in an industry littered with broken ones.

The Call

In this atmosphere the leaders called for a ballot to give the Executive the power to call a strike. The result was a record 81 per cent in favour. The developments from there form part of another story. The purpose of this one has been to show the value of the overtime ban as a tactical weapon. The flow chart opposite underlines this point.

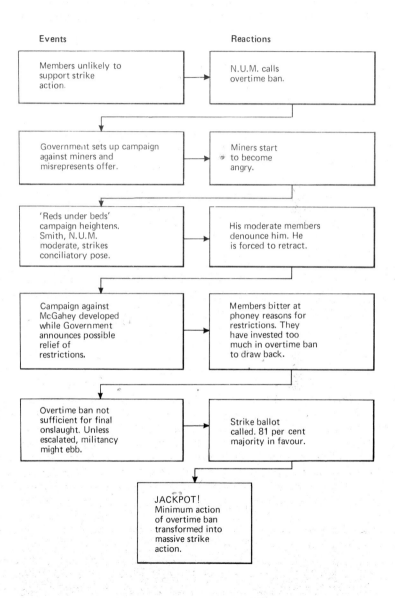

Events   Reactions

Members unlikely to support strike action.

N.U.M. calls overtime ban.

Government sets up campaign against miners and misrepresents offer.

Miners start to become angry.

'Reds under beds' campaign heightens. Smith, N.U.M. moderate, strikes conciliatory pose.

His moderate members denounce him. He is forced to retract.

Campaign against McGahey developed while Government announces possible relief of restrictions.

Members bitter at phoney reasons for restrictions. They have invested too much in overtime ban to draw back.

Overtime ban not sufficient for final onslaught. Unless escalated, militancy might ebb.

Strike ballot called. 81 per cent majority in favour.

JACKPOT! Minimum action of overtime ban transformed into massive strike action.

The Overtime Ban Against Unemployment

Who would argue against the principle that it is wrong for overtime to be worked when unemployment abounds? Why then did the A.U.E.W. Liverpool District Committee in 1972 fail in its attempts to ban all overtime until the employers agreed to take on more labour?

The action began in 1972 when the District Committee called a meeting of shop stewards and branch representatives to consider the growing unemployment on Merseyside. The meeting's recommendation to ban overtime in the district was approved by the District Committee and all stewards were informed that no overtime would be worked without the District Committee's approval.

Managements acted quickly. When some maintenance men threatened to ban overtime, they were told that if machines were broken down, no one could work on them. Production workers were told that banning overtime would create bottlenecks and threaten the existing workers on other sections. This was crude but effective propaganda.

In many factories, management action was not even needed. The workers simply ignored union instructions. The District Committee's authority was only recognized in order to destroy its policy. Excuses poured out, pointing out that all manner of overtime was essential to prevent an even higher level of unemployment.

The District Committee was left with a banner torn to shreds. The final defeat came when one lone steward was removed by his members for insisting on carrying out the policy in full. The Committee refused to accept his removal, but he insisted that he could not carry on without the workers' confidence.

The District Committee was left powerless and ignored, but why? No one can guarantee victory, but failure to perform elementary actions is almost certain to lead to defeat.

The Liverpool District Committee did not think out and carry out a plan of action. For instance, they failed to:

1. Develop a campaign prior to the ban.
2. Consider the likely response of management.
3. Call for the support of other unions.
4. Call factory gate meetings with delegates from the Committee explaining policy.
5. Hold a mass demonstration against unemployment.

6. Consider the membership's level of consciousness.

7. Understand that workers don't respond to matters of principle automatically. This needs hard work.

It is essential that we recognize the value of such lessons if we wish to be successful when we take similar action.

Working to Rule

Working to rule, going slow or working without enthusiasm, call it what you like, is still a weapon which makes the employer howl 'Unfair', 'Not playing the game', or something else which means that you are hurting him more than he cares to admit.

There are probably as many variations of the work-to-rule as there are jobs in industry, so that to look at one case history would not demonstrate very much. For that reason, it is better to understand the effects. Here are some facts.

The price an employer sells his product at is based on two factors: fixed costs (F.C.), plus variable costs (V.C.).

Fixed costs are such things as rent, interest payments, heating, lighting, profits, etc. Variable costs are, in this example, taken as just the wages of the direct labour employed, for the sake of simplicity in this case, three workers.

$$\text{Normal output} = 120 \text{ products per week, each}$$
$$\text{selling at £1·00}$$
$$= £120·00$$
$$\text{Wages (V.C.)} = £90·00$$
$$\text{Overheads (F.C.) and profits} = £30·00$$

Then work-to-rule is imposed. Production falls to thirty articles, but workers' wages (V.C.) only fall to £75 (in all) because their payments system guarantees them a minimum wage of £25·00 each.

The cost of the products under work-to-rule conditions is:

$$\text{V.C.} + \text{F.C.} = £105·00 \text{ for 30 products}$$

As the employer cannot raise his selling price, he is losing £75·00 per week. The three workers, however, only lose £5·00 a week each. Compare with this the cost of the strike as opposed to the work-to-rule. The employer during a strike loses only his fixed costs, £30·00. The workers lose all their wages.

In the example it is assumed that the employer can reduce the workers' wages to a minimum rate. He cannot always do this, for instance when workers are on straight time-rates. Nor is a work-to-rule open only to direct workers. Indirect workers can, by going slow, drastically reduce the material fed to the direct workers, delay the tools required, slow the progress of work from one stage to another and delay the delivery of finished products. Service industries too, are by no means immune, as the A.S.L.E.F. dispute (January 1974) shows. Public services can be delayed and even halted by a work-to-rule.

There are, of course, serious drawbacks:

1. The worker is much more susceptible to management propaganda.

2. The employer will not tolerate for long the situation described in the example. You will soon find yourself locked out (as during the Lucas site trouble; see Chapter 1). With some careful planning, though, the action can be pitched at a level that is just costing the employer more than it would to settle.

3. Always remember that the boss will find any way he can to pressurize you and other activists. BEWARE!

SOURCES

1. *The Miner*, January and February 1974.
2. Minutes of the A.U.E.W. Liverpool District Committee, 1972.

4 Who's in Charge?

The Sit-In

The impetus for the recent increase in the use of this weapon was almost certainly the success of the U.C.S. work-in. The sit-in is not, however, new. For instance, it was used in America in the 1930s to secure union recognition.

In its recent rebirth, apart from the Manchester sit-ins, it has been deployed mostly against closures and the threat of closures unless drastic remanning took place.

In the present period capitalism is rationalizing its productive forces. The results are closed factories, with thousands thrown out of work, and demands for remanning. All this happens with little regard to the rights of the cast-off workers.

The sit-in, when it is used to demonstrate the right to work, is the workers' blunt way of saying to the employer: 'We deny your right to do as you want with your property at our expense.'

The more 'normal' strike is of little avail against a closure. It simply removes an unwanted work force from the factory. Short of political action, the sit-in and the work-in are probably the only weapons open to the workers. The sit-in throws the management out of the factory and denies the owners the use of their property as a marketable asset. Thus the factory becomes a powerful bargaining point and puts the workers temporarily in charge.

The advantages of a sit-in as compared to strike action are shown in table form overleaf.

The two sit-ins at Fisher Bendix, Kirkby, and at C.A.V., Faza-kerley, have been chosen for consideration because one was a success, and the other a failure. The reasons cannot be explained by the usual pat answer that one area was more militant than the other, for the factories stand four miles apart. Both factories faced closure and had run at a loss for some years, but there were differences between them. All the Fisher Bendix work was to be transferred elsewhere, while 40 per cent of the C.A.V. work was

Problems Arising	Advantage of Sit-In	Advantage of Strike
1. Availability of management information	Much information comes into workers' hands after opening confidential files (which should never have been confidential).	Little or none
2. Scabs	None inside factory	Depends on effective picketing
3. Picketing	What is needed at the factory can be done from inside (where it is warmer and drier), removing police threats to pickets. *Watch out though,* since picketing of other places to get products blacked may be needed. So you're not immune.	Questionable, since the strike is always vulnerable to police harassment
4. Morale	Concerts, films, etc., shown in the factory raise morale.	Little chance of raising workers' morale other than at mass meetings
5. Workers' involvement	A much higher percentage of workers take part, raising their consciousness.	Little, since the strike is nearly always left to the stewards and a few activists
6. Strike committee rooms	Ready-made in factory office blocks. Management might cut off supplies, but experience shows that these are almost always restored through fear of damage to property.	Often difficult to obtain near to the factory
7. Bargaining power	Increased through challenge to property rights and holding finished products	Depends on the issue. If it is a closure, there is almost no bargaining power.
8. Publicity	Certainly the sit-in seems to get more than a strike does, but this may be because of its novelty.	Depends on the issue

obsolete. Also, C.A.V. was one of two factories on one site. This was a matter of some importance, as things turned out.

The Fisher Bendix Sit-In

Redundancy

In May 1971 Thorn Electric, of which Fisher Bendix was a subsidiary, stated to their workers that 'the Thorn Group is well known to enjoy excellent human relations at all levels.' In June they announced plans to sack 450, that is, half of the factory's labour force. The workers reacted with a nine-week strike, which made management withdraw its redundancy notices and promise to re-examine the position.

Closure

In December management announced that the factory would be run down and closed by May, because of falling markets and consistent losses. All the washing machine production had been transferred to Spain during the strike. Workers were instructed, on threat of dismissal, to dismantle the equipment used for the making of domestic and storage heaters, ready for its transfer to Newcastle and Birmingham. These threats were issued alongside a statement that 'the Thorn Management is proud of its record for growth and sustained employment.'

Sitting In

After negotiations to keep the factory open had failed, the workers occupied it on 5 January 1972. As one worker said, 'Far better to stay inside and hold on to the plant than see it going through thin picket lines.'

The Combine Committee

The stewards acted quickly. All workers and staff, up to and including foremen, joined the sit-in. The Liverpool dockers resumed, at the stewards' request, the total blacking of Thorn's goods which had taken place during the strike. The managers had taken up residence at a local hotel. They were evicted after a

deputation put it to the owner that his trade might suffer. Thus, management's line of communication with the factory was stretched as far as possible. No combine committee existed, so the stewards formed one. Its first meeting took place in the board room at the factory, with delegates from Birmingham, Merthyr, Leicester, Bradford, Bromley and Enfield, as well as the Kirkby factory. This resolution was carried unanimously: 'That the Thorn Combine Committee endorse the action taken . . . and pledge solidarity and will inform their respective managements of this resolution.'

Keeping Up Morale

To quote Jack Spriggs, the A.U.E.W. convenor: 'All the workers responded magnificently. This was met with an equal response from other workers, both in this district and throughout the country. The sit-in committee helped keep up morale with different kinds of entertainment and the need for discipline was stressed continuously.' Visits were made to the U.C.S. work-in and the Plessey sit-in and the reports raised the spirits of the workers.

The Management Retreat

During the partial blacking of Thorn's goods and with a total black developing, Harold Wilson, M.P. for the constituency, chaired a meeting at which nine points were drawn up as the basis for keeping the factory open. The main points were: 'that the factory remain open until at least the end of 1973'; and 'that a working party of both sides examine the need to keep the existing work force employed, even to the point of finding a new tenant for part of the premises.' On this basis a return to work took place on 7 February 1972.

What was significant was that management was now forced to hold more honest talks with the workers, and even went as far as opening the books. Yet doubts were still being held about the viability of the factory and the minutes of the working party were studded with hints of an unknown prospective tenant. At the fifteenth meeting of the working party, he was revealed as a Mr King.

A New Owner

Although it was clear by 20 March that all the jobs were safe it was not until 1 April that an agreement was drawn up. Thorn sold their interests to International Property Developments (I.P.D.), of which King was chairman. Though the title suggests that King was a property speculator, he 'wanted in' on the manufacturing business and guaranteed to run the factory as a production unit.

Patience

The workers had to pay a price. They agreed that they would take no industrial action and make no claims on wages or conditions for six months. But they felt they needed a breather anyway, and the time could be well spent consolidating the unity built during the sit-in.

Victory

After the standstill period the workers negotiated the shortest hours for engineering in the district: a 36-hour, 4½-day week, and a night-shift of 28½ hours. They became some of the highest paid workers in the area and the labour force was increased by four hundred. Here are the real signs of the unity developed during the sit-in.

The C.A.V. Sit-In

A Shot Across the Bows

Twelve months before the announced closure a redundancy took place at C.A.V., and was accepted against the stewards' advice. The first test of the workers' stamina showed that there was little resistance. From then until September 1972 rumours circulated about the future of the factory. By September the rumours had strengthened that Simms, a recently acquired firm in the Lucas Combine, was to take over 40 per cent of the work done at C.A.V. Fazakerley with its product. A visit by the C.A.V. stewards to the Simms Finchley factory confirmed this.

Double-cross

The management agreed to talk to the stewards about the factory's future. However, on the day before the meeting a letter was handed to each worker saying that the factory would close by April 1973. The reasons given were the heavy losses over the years and that much of the work was obsolete.

When key workers were induced to leave, it seemed doubtful whether the factory would remain open until April. Machine operators found that they could not book on to their jobs because management had talked booking clerks into taking their redundancy money and going. Faced with this, the workers met on 4 October and carried an almost unanimous decision to sit-in. Despite this, almost half the workers left there and then, leaving about 450 to proceed.

The First Blunder

Management told the press that the work force of 1100 had occupied the factory. The workers thought that this was good propaganda and fell for it. It is extremely doubtful whether more than 900 workers were employed by C.A.V. at that time. Certainly not more than half this number sat in. The management was able to announce week by week the falling numbers engaged in the sit-in. Meanwhile, the workers were powerless, unless they admitted that they had been parties to cooking the original figures. All this gave the impression that the sit-in was losing support.

Double Trouble

C.A.V. and Lucas shared the same site (see Chapter 1). While C.A.V. sat in, Lucas worked on. When the C.A.V. workers asked other factories and the dockers to black all Lucas goods, they were asked why the Lucas factory was still working. In the fourth week of the sit-in the C.A.V. workers decided to occupy the whole site and lock out the Lucas workers, in order to get support for a general blacking of Lucas goods.

Transport

Another reason which decided the workers to occupy the site was that all goods sent from other Lucas factories outside Merseyside were delivered to Fazakerley first and then transported to the local Lucas and car factories. The occupation of the site imprisoned the Fazakerley fleet and the Birmingham drivers refused to deliver direct to Liverpool factories. This was overcome by the Birmingham drivers unwittingly delivering extra supplies to Fords, Dagenham, which were sent by rail and internal Ford transport to the Halewood factories. The unpalatable fact is that the workers at other Lucas Merseyside factories, Fords and Standards, all refused to black Lucas parts.

The Dockers

The dockers argued that if they were to black Lucas goods they would have to black almost all cars on which other workers had fitted Lucas equipment. According to those involved in the sit-in the dockers were more frightened by the £55000 fine imposed on their union in April 1972 and the possible repercussions if they blacked Lucas products. It appears that this was indeed a major reason for the lack of response from the dockers.

Dispute Benefit

When support began to fall away among those sitting in, it

became difficult to know who were just not turning up for their shifts and who had taken redundancy money. Management did not talk. This caused much discontent. The A.U.E.W. rules certainly need changing to relate dispute benefit to the action being taken. Bluntly, in a sit-in, if you sit at home and not in the factory you shouldn't get benefit.

The London Trip

Word came to the sit-in committee that work normally done at Fazakerley was being done at Finchley. Two delegates were sent to London to meet a national officer who was responsible for Finchley. He was in a meeting when they arrived so they decided there were more important things to do than wait for an official to come out of a meeting. They left. Meanwhile, the work continued to be done at Finchley.

Isolated

The Executive Council were refusing to call a meeting of delegates from all Lucas factories and support was dwindling at local level. The C.A.V. workers were left isolated. The Lucas workers were demanding more and more pressingly that the occupation of the site should end; they were threatened with the closure of their factory too if the sit-in did not end. This developed into threats by the Lucas workers to break down the gates. After twenty weeks the sit-in ended and the 250 workers left accepted defeat.

The Broken Agreement

Among the minimum conditions the workers won was an agreement that they should get priority when vacancies occurred in the local Lucas factories. Within four months, workers who had been prominent in the sit-in committee were still unemployed, but Lucas bypassed them and employed fresh labour. The A.U.E.W. District Committee's only response was that 'Such an agreement could not last for ever.'

So ended the defeat of the C.A.V. sit-in. It was also a major defeat for Merseyside, because much of the work which was moved away went to Fascist Spain.

Questions

What events in these two sit-ins led to the success of one and the failure of the other?

Some pertinent questions may provide the answers.

1. Was there a redundancy prior to the closure notice?

Fisher Bendix: Yes, and it was fought successfully. This created a united work force.

C.A.V.: Yes, but the workers did not fight. This caused mass desertion before the sit-in began.

Lesson: Never accept any redundancy.

2. Was timing important?

Answer: Yes, the £55000 fine of the T.G.W.U. fell between these two sit-ins, resulting in C.A.V. not getting the support from the dockers which Fisher Bendix received.

Lesson: The Industrial Relations Act needed repealing.

3. Was there any important difference between the two situations?

Answer: Yes, Fisher Bendix was a single factory site. C.A.V. was a two-factory site, which allowed management to play one group of workers off against the other.

Lesson: Workers must learn they cannot safeguard their interests at the expense of others.

4. Was there a problem with dispute benefit?

Fisher Bendix: No.

C.A.V.: Yes, workers not sitting in claimed and got dispute benefit.

Lesson: Dispute benefit must be related to the action taken. Union rules must spell this out.

5. How did the workers respond to managerial propaganda?

Fisher Bendix: The stewards analysed all of management statements and issued factual replies.

C.A.V.: The stewards accepted management's figures on the labour force. Thereafter new management statements suggested that support for the sit-in was falling off.

Lesson: Never accept management statements. Analyse them. Give the correct position or refuse to comment.

6. Were delegations carried out effectively?

Fisher Bendix: Yes.

C.A.V.: No. For example, one group refused to wait for a national official who was in a meeting.

Lesson: Make sure duties are carried out. The final solution is to get rid of dead wood.

7. Was local and national leadership adequate?

Fisher Bendix: It was seldom called on.

C.A.V.: Little leadership was given. The national leaders refused to call a meeting of all Lucas stewards throughout the country. There was little sign of local officials at the factory when they were needed.

Lesson: Demand support. Don't hesitate to invade the citadels of power with your demands.

8. Were there any problems after the sit-in ended?

Fisher Bendix: Yes. There were signs that the unity created during the sit-in was breaking up, but all the stewards joined in to overcome this by analysing how the unity was created and agreeing on a future common policy.

C.A.V.: Yes. Too many people refused to accept responsibility for the failure. There was no real analysis of the reasons for the failure. Also the District Committee refused to honour their agreement on the employment of those made redundant.

Lesson: Insist on a balanced analysis. It is vital that in the future others do not repeat your mistakes. Also, never permit agreements to be ratted on. Use the appeals procedure of your union, if necessary.

9. Any other points?

Answer: Yes, above all, never underestimate the employers. They learn from their mistakes too and develop new tactics to beat you.

SOURCES

1. Minutes and documents of Fisher Bendix sit-in.
2. Minutes of the Fisher Bendix working party.
3. Minutes and documents of C.A.V. sit-in.
4. Minutes of the A.U.E.W. Liverpool District Committee, 1972–3.

5 The Militant Works On

The Work-In

The work-in not only strikes at the employer's property rights, by stopping him from realizing the property's value, but it also uses the property to continue manufacturing in the workers' interests.

At this stage of trade union development it is doubtful if it can be used effectively other than in the defensive fight for the right to work. Even at this level it is difficult to handle. The U.C.S. work-in is now internationally famous and has become an inspiration to others. Yet the U.C.S. workers had advantages that other workers did not have. This may be why those inspired by U.C.S. opt mainly for the sit-in rather than the work-in.

Let us then look at the essentials of the U.C.S. work-in and compare them with Triumph Meriden.

The Upper Clyde Work-In

Liquidation

The story begins in June 1972 with U.C.S. consisting of three divisions, Govan, Clydebank and Scotstoun. The Government, having refused a £6 million loan, appointed a special committee, which eventually consisted of four men, to report on the future of U.C.S. The committee found that the only practical solution was that U.C.S. should go into liquidation. The Clydebank and Scotstoun divisions should close and the Govan division should stay open only if the workers accepted double day-shift working and 'competitive wage rates'.

The Social Cost

In human terms this meant that the U.C.S. work force would be reduced from 8500 to 2500. The real effects went much deeper than this. There were sub-contractors and other small businesses on the Clyde whose life blood depended on U.C.S. If the Government's policy was carried out it meant that as many as 20000 would be on the dole.

Michael Barratt Brown (in Workers' Control *Pamphlet* No. 26) estimated the cost in unemployment benefit due to this policy. The benefit to be paid over three years on the basis of reducing the percentage of unemployed would be as follows:

Starting at 5000 unemployed, the cost = £3·14 million
Starting at 27000 unemployed, the cost = £16·93 million

Barratt Brown also estimated the cost of resettling the unemployed in places where there were jobs. His figures were as follows:

To resettle 5000 costs £32·25 million
To resettle 15000 costs £96·75 million

Is it any wonder that the Clyde saw the refusal to keep the yards open with a loan of £6 million as an attack on the whole community, particularly when unemployment in the area was already high?

The Workers Prepare

Preparations to fight the closures were well under way long before the Government accepted the Committee's findings. A one-day stoppage was called on 24 June. Throughout the West of Scotland 100000 stopped work; 50000 demonstrated in Glasgow. So support from other workers was won.

Why a work-in? The leaders felt that this was going to be a long fight, so that a sit-in covering four separate yards would demoralize the workers and cause desertions. The plan of the work-in was that those made redundant should stay at work and be paid from funds collected to support them. The two most important parts of the strategy were that:

1. Working on meant that they were exposing the obscenity of unemployment.

2. They would become the makers of the decisions if and when completed ships would be released; this was a most powerful bargaining weapon.

The Work-In Starts

On 30 June, the day after the Government pronounced the official death sentence of the U.C.S., the work-in began. Every man in the yards agreed to a levy of 50p each week to swell the wages fund for those made redundant but staying at work. There was considerable backing from the whole of the local community. This soon spread and cash rolled in from all over Britain and even international sources.

A coordinating committee was set up and six places were given to middle management and staff workers, which was most important. This created a united work force. Committees under the control of the coordinating committee looked after finance, publicity, administration and entertainment.

On 18 August another token strike and a demonstration took place. These even overshadowed the predecessor; 200000 stopped work and 80000 demonstrated. Thus the determination of the workers and support for them were stepped up.

Behind this high tempo there was much hard work and organization by the coordinating committee to keep a disciplined work-in going.

Highlights of Policy

Through constant reference to the workers the committee created the following policy:

1. No overtime unless on essential maintenance.
2. No booze in the yards.
3. No extra output when redundant men go to work with their mates.
4. All opinions must be given the right to be heard.
5. No statements on finance. The enemy must not know the strength or weakness of the fighting fund.
6. No dogma. The right to work was the struggle. All feasible offers for employing all the work force in the existing yards on shipbuilding should be considered.

The Big Decision

The struggle continued until January when union officials went to America to discuss the possibility that the Clydebank division might be taken over by American interests. Against this background, the *New Westminster City*, the first ship ready for delivery since the work-in began, lay in the Govan yard. Should she be released? The coordinating committee was divided; the majority suspected that the Government was ready to pounce and declare the U.C.S. stewards 'wreckers', frightening off prospective American buyers. The workers endorsed the decision to release the ship and the Government's attack was forestalled.

All's Well

By February, the Government had retreated, prepared to incorporate the Scotstoun yard into a new company called Govan Shipbuilding Ltd., backed by £35 million public money. With this went an offer of assistance for any buyer of Clydebank, which was soon taken up by American interests. Though months of negotiations lay ahead to work out final details, the work-in had succeeded in its objective of saving the jobs of all those who refused to accept redundancy. Even more important, a whole community was saved from depression.

The Triumph Meriden Work-In

The Merger

An important part of this story is one that is all too common with closures. Mergers take place, Government grants are obtained and then both workers and public interests ignored. Norton Villiers Triumph was formed in July 1973 with the help of £4·8 million of public money. It was, in fact, the rump of a once thriving motor-cycle industry.

The Work-In

In September 1973 R. D. Poore, Chairman of N.V.T. and director of its parent company Manganese Bronze, announced closure plans for the Meriden works and the transfer of production to the Small Heath factory in Wolverhampton.

On 2 October the workers placed a blockade on all bikes, jigs, fixtures and machinery and the work-in began. There followed a series of marathon discussions. The workers offered one bike out of the works for one new order placed at the factory. Always management seemed reasonble at first, and then went back on what had previously been said.

The Workers' Cooperative

One of the most important developments was the idea of setting up a workers' cooperative. Again, after much 'Now we will, now we won't', the management seemed to go along with the idea.

Money Trouble

At first the cooperative was to be based on labour only. N.V.T. would pay a fixed price for each finished bike and the proceeds would be shared among the workers. Later, the option to buy outright was to be open to the workers, but on 2 February 1974 the management refused to ratify the agreement, claiming that the cash for supplies could not be afforded. Yet American dealers said that there was a genuine market for the bikes in their country.

Developments

Anthony Wedgwood-Benn, the Minister responsible in the Labour Government, made Government money forthcoming to help the new cooperative. Out of a total labour force of 1750 no more than 375 were left.

The Most Important Lessons and Questions

U.C.S.

1. The leaders of the work-in fought for and won the support of not only the workers involved but of the whole community.

2. By winning the support of the Govan workers whose jobs seemed more secure, they prevented one group being played off against the other. (Contrast this with the C.A.V. Lucas situation.)

3. They allowed all views to be expressed, thus avoiding 'big brother' tactics.

4. The size and value of the ships they controlled was most important for bargaining with.

5. They won the support of middle management and staff, making room for them on the coordinating committee.

6. They were flexible and distinguished principles from tactics. For instance, they released the *New Westminster City* to prevent adverse publicity.

7. Discipline was excellent. Not one person was killed or injured throughout the work-in.

8. They kept to clear limited objectives. Their aim was to keep the yards open, not to indulge in preconceived ideas such as nationalization, which is another battle.

Triumph Meriden

1. They fought almost as an isolated unit. No real help came from other workers in the Manganese Bronze combine.

2. The only reference by Meriden workers to the Small Heath factory seemed to be: 'We can do the job better than them.' Compare this with U.C.S.'s winning of the Govan workers.

3. Over half the labour force left. Did this indicate a serious split?

4. Compared with the total assets of the parent company, was the value of what they were blockading of vital importance?

5. Discipline was excellent, with no damage to plant, etc.

6. Did they enter into a dogmatic stand that the cooperative was the *only* solution?

POSTSCRIPT

The general view of those on the left who doubt the success of the Triumph Meriden experiment is that a workers' cooperative is bound to fail because big business would not tolerate an island of socialism in a sea of capitalism. It is, of course, a valid point. But it seems to have succeeded and may well survive. A Labour Government at least made it possible. It can be argued that if the workers save their jobs that is all that matters. Is it? Equally important is the possibility that the cooperative might take on the features of the capitalist system which surrounds it and lose all identity with the labour movement. What would be the point in the workers belonging to a union when they are their own employer? This is the blackest side of the picture, and these are the real dangers. On the bright side, the workers at Triumph Meriden, with a really developed political consciousness and a dedication to winning people over, can rally workers to the cause.

SOURCES

1. 'The Social Audit', Institute of Workers' Control *Pamphlet* No. 26.
2. Willie Thompson and Finlay Hart, *The U.C.S. Work-In*, Lawrence & Wishart, 1972.
3. Institute of Workers' Control *Bulletins*: November 1973; no. 7, January 1974; no. 9, February 1974; no. 13, March 1974.

6 Picketing

Your Rights?

It is almost certain that sit-ins and work-ins are illegal. Even if, as has been argued, the workers have a licence by being employees to be on the premises, the employer has only to sack them to put them beyond the law. Why has the media, usually so keen on law and order, given little publicity to the legal position of sit-ins and work-ins?

Sharston Engineering sought possession of their factory from nineteen sacked workers. In 1972 during the Manchester sit-ins Sir Thomas Burgess in the Chancery Court in Preston granted a writ of possession. He showed some concern, though, when he said: 'This is a small firm and it would be possible for a small number of people to get them out. If it was a big factory, you might want two thousand policemen with tear gas. I want to make sure that any order I might make can be enforced.' It is not then what the law says but what can be enforced which is important. Few employers would risk the serious damage that pitched battles in their factories would cause.

Picketing is different. We should be concerned with the law here, not because it is immoral to break it but because too often it is fairly easy for the police to impose it. It is essential to establish that if withholding labour by collective action is a democratic right, then picketing to support that action is equally a basic civil liberty.

Being Good Boys

If you carry out the letter of the law your picketing is likely to be completely ineffective. This raises serious problems. If we are to overcome unjust laws then we need to do so effectively. A small picket line out for an adventure with the police will achieve nothing but its own downfall. Yet a small picket line is sometimes unavoidable. For example, your union may insist on minimum picketing. In such cases, obey the police exactly. You will prove that minimum picketing is useless and escalation vital.

You suddenly find yourselves pushed unexpectedly into a strike. Time is needed to build up a strong picket line. Don't hesitate to be friendly with the police in these circumstances. In this way you will gain time to build a strong picket line. But always warn the pickets that the honeymoon will only last until management complains that you are being too effective.

Friendly Persuasion

The police may try to limit the number of pickets. In 1968, during a strike, a 'boy in blue' with pips on his shoulder told us that our eighteen pickets were too many. A glance at the eight policemen convinced us there was little point in arguing. At the mass meeting the next day we told the thousand workers present of the new orders. One lad, well briefed beforehand, moved that half the workers stay and form a mass picket to be relieved later by the other half. The resolution was carried and the 'boy in blue' asked us to behave reasonably. However, we soon reached agreement on thirty pickets, because eighteen did not seem enough to deal with emergencies. A word of warning: make sure the mover of such resolutions is well hidden in the crowd and never name him. The police can, and do, act against such people.

Some Basic Hints

1. Keep your picket line tidy. Nothing looks worse or is more damaging to discipline than an untidy line.

2. Keep your posters to the point and well displayed.

3. Make sure everyone obeys the picket marshals. Those who won't must go.

4. No beer. Quite apart from disciplinary reasons, a harmless 'empty' can become an offensive weapon.

5. Avoid tiredness. Change your pickets regularly.

6. Find a sympathetic solicitor. All pickets should know his phone number.

7. Instruct all pickets of their right to make one phone call if arrested. Tell everyone to say 'No comment', unless a solicitor is present.

8. The National Council of Civil Liberties issues brief but useful

pamphlets. Their address is 152 Camden High St, London NW1 0NN.

The Mass Picket

Effective picket lines help to win strikes. However, in most strikes many workers think that their job is done once they have come out. In the long run the crucial task is to raise the consciousness of the workers until they realize that they must all work to help win the strike. Until this is achieved we must live in the world as it is. The mass picket is one way of overcoming the problem of sparse picket lines.

Roberts Arundel

In the case of Roberts Arundel, Stockport, the sparse picket line was caused by the small number of workers involved in the strike. This was a serious matter, considering the seriousness of the issue.

In November 1966, 145 workers walked out because the firm had broken a national agreement. Events were to prove that the employers wanted no truck with trade unionism at any cost. They resigned from the Employers' Federation rather than honour national agreements.

The strike eventually developed into a struggle to close the factory rather than let it be a haven of non-unionism. It became impossible, in the face of a vicious management and a first unsympathetic and later antagonistic police force, for 145 workers to keep an effective 24-hour picket on the factory.

Bill Anton, the District President of the A.U.E.W. in Stockport as well as a Labour Councillor, was arrested during a demonstration against the Roberts Arundel management on 18 February 1967. His arrest ensured support for the mass picket of the factory planned for 22 February. Six hundred Stockport workers gathered that day outside the factory. A mile away hundreds of workers got off buses which had brought them from the Shell Carrington site. They marched the mile to the factory determined to be rid of it as well as the scabs inside. To quote from Jim Arnison's *The Million Pound Strike*, 'The most awful sound I have ever heard came through the mist, just one word repeated over and over – OUT, OUT . . . OUT, OUT, OUT.'

The mass picket got out of hand, perhaps inevitably, because of the reports of increasing police hostility and Anton's arrest. Order was restored by Johnny Tocher, the A.U.E.W. District Secretary. Other demonstrations took place near the factory later in the strike but from the time of the mass picket of 22 February, the Roberts Arundel workers were assured of two things:

1. Constant support on the picket line from other trade unionists.
2. Undreamed-of publicity and probings into the cause of the strike.

Without the mass picket and demonstrations, it is doubtful if the strike would have been won.

After the mass picket, police arrests and physical assaults on the pickets increased, in spite of rigid discipline. Be warned: no matter how careful you are, you still take grave risks on a picket line.

The Flying Picket

This is a valuable way of ensuring that thinly manned picket lines can be supplemented at a suitable moment. Flying pickets gained popularity during the 1972 miners' strike. The tactic was that large groups of pickets would descend on places such as power stations and coal tips by coach and car. Caught by surprise, the police were far outnumbered. By motorizing their pickets the miners were able to hit at the most important strategic points. In fact, they moved away from their traditional strategy of picketing pit heads only. Such was the effectiveness that the police did not know where they would hit next. These tactics, of course, required the utmost coordination and secrecy. If the police know about their intentions, their effect would be ruined, because reasons can be found to stop coaches or cars from reaching the intended place of action.

Conspiracy

In the 1973 building workers' strike, it was not the much hated Industrial Relations Act which was invoked against flying pickets. Instead, action was taken under the Conspiracy and Protection of Property Act (1875). Of course, no one was charged with being a member of a squad of flying pickets. The charges levelled against the Shrewsbury Two were that they conspired to indulge in criminal activities.

The reason for not using the Industrial Relations Act against these lads was probably the storm of protest which arose out of using it against the Pentonville Five.

Cleverly, no action was taken against any building workers while they were on strike. The police acted after the dispute had ended and men had gone back to their building sites, when the unity created during the strike was dissolving.

The big problem has been that the charge is a criminal rather than a civil one, as it would have been under the Industrial Relations Act. There has been much debate in trade union circles about how best to help them. The trade union movement has failed to give those imprisoned the support they deserve and need.

There is a great danger that since the repeal of the Industrial Relations Act, pickets will still be treated as criminals under the 1875 Act. Nor can any great comfort be taken from the case of the two A.P.E.X. members, Ed Murphy and Bert Dickinson, who were charged under the 1875 Act and got off. The police on behalf of the courts are clearly testing on what grounds pickets can be defined as criminals.

Unless the movement is prepared to support people like the Shrewsbury Two, picketing may become a way to martyrdom instead of a way to help win strikes.

At the moment, the only safety seems to be in numbers. A determined effort must be made to make the union leaders fight with industrial weapons the injustice to the Shrewsbury Two.

The strike called by the A.U.E.W. against the sequestration of all their assets by the Industrial Relations Court forced the repeal of the Industrial Relations Act. The 1875 Act should be amended to prevent pickets being treated as criminals.

Finally, pickets must be given *positive* rights which not only protect them but also allow them to do their job effectively.

SOURCES

1. 'The Right to Govern', Cardiff University case study, unpublished.
2. J. Arnison, *The Million Pound Strike*, Lawrence & Wishart, 1971.
3. A.P.E.X. *Journal*, December 1973.

7 Some Thorny Problems

In this chapter we will look at three major problems facing trade unionists: disputes between unions, the strike against the union, and the strike promoted by the employer. All three are important because, unless we are aware of them, we might be caught napping and find ourselves acting against our own interests.

Disputes Between Unions

This is one of the biggest causes of trouble among unions today. It sets worker against worker, creates opposing policies and smashes the chances of a unified work force.

The Chrysler Dispute, Coventry, August 1973

This was a classic illustration of the destructive forces created by rows between unions.

The strike by the E.E.T.P.U. to eliminate existing differentials between electricians and toolroom workers resulted in a souring of relations which still persists.

Whatever the rights or wrongs of the electricians' claim, it is a fact that the A.U.E.W. and the T.G.W.U. committed two unpardonable acts: they crossed picket lines, and they worked with blackleg labour.

These issues are not only important at the time, but they create an atmosphere which lasts, because when a problem next comes along which needs maximum unity of action, each side points to the other's past for reasons for not joining together.

There are no easy solutions, but here are a few hints which may help.

1. Never scab against another union. No one listens to a scab.
2. Remember temporary advantages won at another union's expense help no one but management in the long run.

3. Never take unilateral action without the fullest and frankest talks with other unions.

4. If your own union representatives instruct you to work with blacklegs or cross picket lines, tell them to go to hell.

The Strike Against the Union, Pilkingtons, 1970

The question of how to deal with undemocratic practices in a union has been debated for a long time. The more sophisticated trade unionists argue that the only way is to fight within the union for reforms. Most workers have learned that forming break-away unions is no answer. This was not the case at Pilkingtons, St Helens, where the General and Municipal Workers Union had sole negotiating rights for process workers, with contributions deducted from wages.

Explosion

On Friday 3 April 1970, forty-five workers stopped work after a wages error had been made for the third week running. By Sunday, all six St Helens factories had stopped. Demands were made for a £10·00 a week increase, and Pilkingtons made an offer of £3·00. However, even joint pressure from the firm and the G.M.W.U. failed to persuade the workers to go back.

Against the G.M.W.U.

By the fourth week of the strike the rank-and-file strike committee (R.F.S.C.), which had been set up in the second week, was beginning to see it as much in terms of a fight against an undemocratic union, as a fight against Pilkingtons. This also seemed to be the view held by many workers who feared being expelled from the G.M.W.U. for even voicing criticism. It became a matter of the G.M.W.U. and some stewards against the R.F.S.C.

The Ballot

Among charges and counter-charges, both sides agreed to a secret ballot on 16 May supervised by local clergy. The result was a majority of 274 in favour of a return to work. The R.F.S.C. hotly disputed the figures and claims were made of ballot rigging. How-

ever, the next Monday 2500 returned to work. After hurried
discussions with the T.U.C., the R.F.S.C. recommended a full
return.

The New Union

Two weeks later the R.F.S.C. handed management 3500 signatures demanding that deductions of contributions to the G.M.W.U.
from wages should cease. However, the R.F.S.C. then found that
the T.G.W.U. would not accept them, so the Glass and General
Workers Union was formed.

In August, a worker was suspended and demanded representation from the G.G.W.U. The management refused on the grounds
that only the G.M.W.U. had negotiating rights. The leaders of the
new G.G.W.U., formed mainly from the old R.F.S.C., called for
a three-day protest strike. Only 480 workers responded. Isolated,
380 were re-employed after signing statements that they were
G.M.W.U. members. The rest were left to rot until they capitulated, and the leaders were blacked.

Analysis

So ended this sorry story. Some interesting things came to light.
An inquiry set up during the strike and chaired by Professor Wood
found: 'That the G.M.W.U. was to be criticized for its inadequate
branch structure and its low level of participation', as was 'the
R.F.S.C. for its lack of mature judgement and sound leadership'.
How was the R.F.S.C. supposed to develop mature judgement and
sound leadership if the G.M.W.U.'s branch structure was inadequate with only a low level of participation? It is more likely
that the lack of democracy in the G.M.W.U. was the direct cause
of the immaturity of the R.F.S.C., and that all the blame rests
with the G.M.W.U.

A further disturbing feature was the ferocity with which the
G.M.W.U. fought the R.F.S.C. compared with the good relations
it had with Pilkingtons, despite, according to the inquiry,
'Pilkingtons' slowness in revising wage structures'.

The International Socialists were at work during the strike,
openly advising the R.F.S.C. to break with the G.M.W.U. and
form a breakaway union. If such groups know no better than to
encourage inexperienced workers to embark on adventurous
actions, then they should keep their advice to themselves.

Warning: always make sure anyone offering help does so your way or not at all.

The Only Way

If the R.F.S.C. had stayed in the G.M.W.U. and campaigned for democratic reforms, the G.M.W.U. would have been hard-pressed not to make some concessions. Expulsion of the rebels would have been difficult for the G.M.W.U. after all the adverse publicity and would have created a case for other unions to insist on their right to enrol the non-unionists, thus breaking the stranglehold of the G.M.W.U. at Pilkingtons.

The Strike Promoted by the Employer

'The Company had decided as a matter of deliberate policy to bring about a situation in which it was hoped that a strike of all operatives would take place and an opportunity be afforded of dismissing the Works Committee as a whole. . . . The events which led to the closing down of their contractual operations at Horseferry Road were the intended result of the deliberate and planned policy of the Directors.'

This quotation is taken from a Government Court of Inquiry, published in September 1967, into disputes at the Barbican and Horseferry Road development sites. The quotation is all the more remarkable because, in general, the inquiry was completely unsympathetic to the stewards.

What is highlighted by this quotation is something which is not uncommon in industry but is seldom commented on: the fact that employers *deliberately* cause strikes. Why? In this case the reason was that Sunley and Sons Ltd. wanted to get out of a contract which had become unprofitable to them. This is by no means the only reason for such actions. Let us look at some others.

1. A factory has a very strong union. The employer has a temporary but heavy fall in orders. He takes advantage of this and provokes the workers into strike action by attacking their conditions or organization, thinking that the action will weaken the workers' solidarity and prevent aggressive action when his order books are full.
2. The situation is the same as in no. 1, but with this difference.

Agreements exist guaranteeing workers minimum wages if they have no work. Such agreements nearly always contain a clause which makes them inoperative if supplies dry up through a dispute in any part of the factory. If the employer can get even a small group of workers to take action, he can then claim that it was the stoppage and not the fall in orders which caused supplies to dry up. He can send the whole work force home and not pay a penny in guaranteed wages.

3. Wages at factory level are very often raised by annual claims which take time to prepare and negotiate. Just when it is clear that you are going to have a fight on your hands to win your claim, management sacks someone and you are forced to defend him, often with a long strike. You may win it but the workers return in no financial state to take on another fight for their wage claim. The employer then has had a strike he would have had to face anyway on the wage issue. He is now, though, in a better position to force you to accept a smaller increase.

The above are perfect examples of the importance of timing emphasized in Chapter 1. This time it is the employer who has timed his action to perfection.

How Do We Overcome This?

Always explain to your members that employers will get up to such tactics. They must know beforehand. All too often shop stewards know what management is up to and they go into the office trying to solve the matter by talking. As they come out of the office they nearly get killed in the rush of workers walking out because lower management have provoked the workers while the stewards were in talking. So workers *must* be aware of management tactics.

In the first two situations, when you are under attack, tell management that agreements are sacred and unbreakable, warning them of the havoc to come when fortunes change, order books are full, and it is *your* turn to break agreements.

In the third situation you have no alternative but to link your wage claim with the reinstatement of the sacked worker. You say that you will not return until *both* demands are met. This way you show management that its tactics are fruitless.

SOURCES

1. E.E.T.P.U. *Journal*, December 1973.
2. 'The Pilkington Dispute', London School of Economics case study.
3. The *Cameron Report*, Cmnd. 3396, H.M.S.O., 1967.

8 Action in the Factory and the Combine

Levels of Action

The case histories we have looked at so far give us an idea of the effectiveness of various types of action. Industrial action, though, is not expressed simply in different forms. It also expresses itself at different levels and for different reasons. We need, then, to look at the levels of industrial action and see in practical terms some of the difficulties facing workers.

Action in the Factory

One of the biggest problems in all action is that of solidarity. Yet solidarity, like charity, must begin at home. Talk of industrial or national unity is pie in the sky unless workers are united in their own workshop. Sometimes, this solidarity is seen at its highest level when workers have had a beating from management and find the only way back from complete managerial dictatorship is to take a stand on trade union principles and fight. In Chapter 1 the convenor of the Lucas site was left in a mess. Let us now look at what happened to him.

Learning the Hard Way

At a mass meeting of the confused and exhausted, as well as the reactionary, the workers were only too willing to accept the result of hurried negotiations between the District Secretary and the management. The convenor was to be suspended on pay while the case went through procedure.

The best elements planned tactics to prevent his ultimate dismissal. The case finally reached national level after one-day token strikes in the strongest departments. Management offered the convenor either six months' pay and the sack or transfer to a small service depot four miles from the factory for twelve months, to be followed by re-employment at the factory. Management complained bitterly about the one-day token strikes. The union asked

for an adjournment for a month for consultations at local level. After these consultations it was agreed to try once more for full reinstatement but all token action had to cease. All token support fell away under this pressure and, ironically, management told the union at the resumed meeting that as all support had now gone, it was not prepared to go further than the original offer.

Putting the Boot In

The convenor accepted the enforced exile and management acted quickly. Another steward was sacked and two more were formally warned. The workers, now completely demoralized, failed to act. Worse was to follow. A demoralized work force saw customs and practices destroyed and deteriorating conditions.

The Light Dawns

After twelve months' exile management refused to take the convenor back into his old factory. He was offered a staff job on another part of the site. The truth was evident: under no circumstances could he hold a job which would entitle him to become convenor again.

The union's Executive now realized that in order to get its own way this management would break an agreement reached at the highest level. The Executive promised support if the members took action. The District Committee called the members at the Lucas factory out on strike and the best elements in the factory argued that to let the management off with this one meant the end of any form of union. The workers were persuaded by this argument and came out, despite management threats that a strike could cause the factory to close permanently. In five weeks the workers were back, having won the greatest victory in the factory's history.

The Workers Lead

Within twelve months of this landmark the stewards were recommending acceptance of management's offer in answer to a wage claim. Previously the workers had at their best supported their stewards' recommendations. Now they did not reject them in a negative way, they simply demanded the claim in full. They were no longer the same people; their stand on trade union principles had changed them. Again, after a strike, they were returning to work having won their full claim.

The workers had learned these valuable lessons:

1. Weakness creates aggressive management.

2. You can only retreat so far. After that the only way out is forward.

3. A principled stand, such as insisting that management will *not* decide who will or will not represent the workers, is the basis of solidarity at its highest level.

4. Having won a principled fight the workers became more aware as trade unionists. As a result they not only supported their stewards, but they could outstrip them in audacity.

Action in the Combine

What is a Combine?

Today workers seldom face an employer who owns a single factory. They find themselves employed by large concerns, who have grouped together many factories under one ownership. Such groupings are known as combines. Nor is this all: few of these combines are isolated in one country. They have burst through the boundaries of the nation state and are multi-national combines with factories all over the world. This makes the problem of workers' solidarity even worse.

What is a Combine Committee?

It is really an extension of the factory shop stewards' committee: members in each factory in a combine send delegates who meet together as a combine committee in order to plan general strategy to fight the combine. In this section, when we speak of the combine we are referring to the employer's side. When we speak of the combine committee, we are referring to the workers' organization.

The Need for Combine Committees

Though solidarity at factory level is vital to success, that is by no means the whole story. Workers acting in the isolation of their own factory and not as part of a combine can find they are negotiating with puppets. The important decisions are made elsewhere and the stewards find themselves unable to reach the real source of power. One way of overcoming this is to do what the Fisher Bendix stewards did: they formed a combine committee and developed coordinated action.

How effective has such coordinated action been? First some cases will be described which show the types of action taken and the successes achieved. Then some of the real difficulties facing workers will be outlined.

The Ford Combine Committee and the 1971 Wage Claim

In February 1971 Ford factories throughout Great Britain voted to join the workers in Halewood and Swansea who had walked out in response to Ford's offer of a £2·00 increase on the basic rate. It was the beginning of a nine-week strike which was to show maximum solidarity between the workers in all the Ford factories in the UK. For example, eighteen days after the strike had begun, the Ford national convenors' meeting needed only the briefest time to decide that the strike was still on. This decision was endorsed by factory gate meetings all over the country. Two weeks later there was exactly the same response to an increased offer of £3·20. Nor were the workers just following the lead the convenors gave them. John Matthews in his book *The Ford Strike* tells the reaction of one factory: 'On Sunday eight hundred Halewood transmission workers decided not to meet for another month – and the platform had a bit of trouble in pushing even this through in the face of shouts from the floor of "Let's not meet again till Christmas".'

The strike was settled after nine weeks with increases of around £8·00 spread over two years, with a threshold clause to cover the cost of living. Even this settlement was resented by many, because the leaders of two major unions took negotiations out of the hands of those normally responsible. Nevertheless, the strike was a measure of real solidarity amongst all the UK Ford factories.

The Dillon Affair

The Ford strike of 1971 certainly expressed workers' solidarity. But it still left a question unanswered. The issue on which they struck had obvious unifying factors: common conditions and wage rates. Everyone clearly stood to gain from united action. Would this solidarity stand up when just one factory is attacked?

The workers at Halewood met with the most abusive tactics that management could devise on their return to work after the nine-week strike. During the strike, supervisors had been holding what Matthews describes as 'hate-ins' in the canteen. The aim? To smash the shop stewards' authority. Workers were disciplined for going to the toilet without permission, work schedules were increased, shop stewards were suspended for allegedly holding meetings, and every attempt was made to prevent stewards representing their members.

The crunch came when the number of workers in the paint shop landing deck had been reduced to an all-time dangerously low level of four men, who were expected to guide red-hot car bodies from overhead ovens on to skips. Enough was enough, down tools, suspension and the entire paint shop walked out. Dillon, their steward, tried to stop the workers from invading the boss's office in the only way he could; he went himself. He was sacked for holding a meeting and leading a demonstration.

All the Ford workers at Halewood stopped work, with the exception of a few skilled men. A meeting of Ford national convenors was called in London; they demanded a strike in all Ford factories. Under this pressure the Halewood strike was made official, and Dillon was reinstated in another part of the factory. This was not a complete victory, but it ended the hate campaign. It also blocked management's aim to destroy the shop stewards' authority at Halewood.

The Ford convenors had shown solidarity to the point of being prepared to call out all their members. Management, however, backed off rather than risk this happening.

In the case of Fords, then, solidarity stood the test even when only one factory was threatened.

Guerrilla Tactics in the Combine

If some workers have organized themselves well within a combine, they can use their forces in the most economic way by withdrawing labour in one factory or area. The members in the rest of the combine can support them by levying themselves.

T.A.S.S. and Rolls-Royce, 1969

In February 1969, the Technical and Supervisory Staff section of the A.U.E.W. lodged a wage claim at the Scottish Rolls-Royce factories. Then they developed guerrilla tactics of token strikes in the Scottish factories. By August the Rolls-Royce offer was still far too low, so a hundred key workers withdrew their labour. This hit the R B 211 engine, which was worth £500 million in exports. Delegates visited Rolls-Royce factories all over the country with the result that other T.A.S.S. members levied themselves. They also visited sub-contractors to Rolls-Royce in Scotland and again T.A.S.S. members levied themselves.

The strikers had hit Rolls-Royce where they were most vulnerable – the R B 211 engine. Finance from other workers ensured there would be no starving out. For their part, the strikers had to be active or produce a doctor's note if they were not fit for strike committee work.

In September, the Scottish workers accepted a £3·00 a week increase back-dated to July. Of the original demand, 75 per cent had been won. Furthermore, similar increases poured through the open floodgates, not only for all T.A.S.S. members in the Rolls-Royce combine but also for T.A.S.S. members in the sub-contracting firms in Scotland.

T.A.S.S. versus Rolls-Royce, 1970

The situation was almost the same as in 1969. The differences were that the place of action was Coventry, and the R B 211 engine was in serious difficulties. This second fact was not known publicly, but it was almost certainly known to some T.A.S.S. members who were working on the technical development of the engine.

Because of the difficulties with the engine, Rolls-Royce was not at all unhappy with the idea of a lock-out. Armed with this threat, management attempted to impose shift-work, timing of jobs and job evaluation as part of the wage settlement. T.A.S.S. were sorepressed to gain what was privately termed 'a hard-fought draw'. The Coventry workers got 43 per cent of their claim. Attempts to impose the conditions Rolls-Royce wanted were resisted. But there was nothing like the same increase in other Rolls-Royce factories.

Lessons

1. The 1969 case shows how effective guerrilla tactics in the combine can be in maximizing results with minimum forces.

2. The 1970 case shows that there is great danger in thinking that any one type of action ensures success. *When* you act can be as important as *how*.

Dunlop Pirelli: the International Strike

The operation of multi-national combines affects the workers of many countries. Such was the case when Dunlop and Pirelli merged in 1971. The plans to merge had been announced two years before. As a result of the merger 8000 jobs in the UK and 1000 in Italy disappeared in the name of rationalization.

With the rumblings of more to come, an international steering committee, consisting of stewards from Italy and the UK, was set up to combat further rationalization at the workers' expense.

The steering committee called for a day of action on 9 June 1972. The Italians planned to stop work for several hours, and the British planned a stoppage of twenty-four hours. Most Italian factories stopped for twenty-four hours because management made difficulties. In all, 25000 Italian and 14000 British workers struck. On the day of action a bilingual newssheet was issued. Workers in two factories in Britain who did not stop on the 9th were so impressed by the solidarity of their comrades that they joined the action later.

The results have been that since the united action there have been no serious labour reductions. Even more important, Dunlop Pirelli made the following concessions to the Italian unions:

1. £20 million should be spent on a new factory in a high unemployment area.

2. Plans to dismiss redundant workers were cancelled.

3. Four hundred redundant workers would be reinstated.

4. The labour force in Italy should be increased by 2200 in the next five years.

Meanwhile in Britain, talks on the same lines went on.

The two main points to make about this action are:

1. A real step towards international unity of workers has taken

place, and workers have achieved what the formal international trade union secretariats have failed to do.

2. Workers have made a major breakthrough in taking from management the sole right in decision-making on any issue concerning the workers' interests, including investment plans.

The Future Role of Combine Committees

Three cases which have shown workers' solidarity in a combine by using different tactics have been examined. The sad truth is that these examples represent an exaggerated picture of combine committee action. In far too many combines, combine committees do not even exist or at best are just talking shops. The reason is that while it is easy for the workers in the three cases we examined to identify with each other because the products they make are similar, often combines make many different products. Workers in a factory making car components do not feel that they have anything in common with a factory making aircraft components just because both factories are owned by the same combine. Yet they do, for it is at the top where the real power lies.

What Can be Done?

Unions must expose the true nature of the combine; members must be provided with the fullest information on how combines destroy workers' unity by paying different wages and operating different conditions.

While we have not yet succeeded on a national level to create unity, the scene has shifted to an international level. The multi-national combine plays one country's workers against another's and makes fat profits out of the game.

In the last chapter it will be seen how the employers realize that they have more in common with employers in other countries than they have with the workers of their own. In the same way, workers must see that their interests are linked with the workers of other countries and not with the employers of their own.

To operate on an international basis we may well need the formal international trade union secretariats which already exist, but workers must learn to make these their servants and not their masters. At the moment some continental unions are barred from joint action with us because they are dominated by Communists.

We must demand an end to discrimination on political grounds. For instance, the democratic loving British employers never refuse to cooperate with Fascist regimes. Unless such fundamental steps as these are taken, the weakest parts of the combine will be used as a threat to the strongest.

SOURCES

1. Minutes of the Lucas Strike Committee, 1968.
2. Minutes of the A.U.E.W. Liverpool District Committee, 1968.
3. Liverpool District Committee and Executive Council letters.
4. John Matthews, *The Ford Strike*, Panther, 1972.
5. Extracts from T.A.S.S. *Journals*, 1969–70.
6. Institute of Workers' Control *Bulletin*, December 1973.
7. Dunlop Pirelli bilingual newssheet, 9 June 1972.

9 Action in One Industry

While workers in some industries are entirely dependent on national negotiations for improvements in wages and conditions, others can do much at factory level and depend on national negotiations only for major changes in conditions, like minimum rates, holidays and hours. Let us look at two important disputes and see the problems endured by the unions concerned.

The Manchester Experiment, 1972

After the Engineering Employers' Federation had offered the Confederation of Shipbuilding and Engineering Unions an increase of £1·50 in answer to a claim for £6·00 on the minimum skilled rate, a 35-hour week and an extra week's holiday, the C.S.E.U. decided that the claim should be pursued at individual factory level with the District Committees coordinating the action.

Though some smaller District Committees did respond to the national call, the only major areas who responded with enthusiasm were the Manchester area and Sheffield (to a lesser extent). This resulted in a small number of workers bearing the brunt of a national claim. This must be borne in mind when considering the final outcome.

How the Sit-Ins Began

The Manchester sit-ins are now famous. They transformed the sit-in from a defensive weapon against redundancy into a positive weapon in support of improved conditions. Yet the sit-ins were not planned; they grew, as we shall see, from management reprisals.

The Manchester Settlements

The C.S.E.U. District Committee in Manchester called a meeting of stewards in their area, at which it was decided that they should push their claim, which was identical to the national one, excetp that they went for increases across the board, they imposed overtime and piecework bans and a work-to-rule. The employers reacted to the workers' sanctions by locking them out. The workers responded by occupying a number of factories and sitting in. Estimates of how many sit-ins took place vary between twenty-seven and forty. A minimum of 8000 workers were involved, though some said that there were as many as 14000. The sit-ins started in March, and some went on until June. Claims were conceded which ranged from £2·00 to £5·00 per week with one or two days' extra holiday. The employers claimed that no more than six or seven firms made concessions over the working week, and these were expelled from the Employers' Federation for doing so. However, the Manchester Divisional Organizer, Johnny Tocher, reported in the A.U.E.W. *Journal* that fifty firms made concessions. The discrepancy is probably because many agreements were made on the basis of no publicity to avoid expulsion.

The National Settlement

Hugh Scanlon, the A.U.E.W. President, toured the country urging that workers in other factories should lodge claims, and so more settlements began to come in until finally the following agreement was reached at national level:

1. No concessions on the working week.
2. Two extra days' holiday.
3. The following rises in minimum rates.

Workers	Old Minimum Rate (£)	Stage 1 (from 26.8.72) New Minimum Rate (£)	Stage 2 (from 25.8.73) New Minimum Rate (£)
Skilled	19·00	22·00	25·00
Unskilled	15·00	17·50	20·00
Women	13·00	15·50	18·00

In percentages the figures represent, in terms of the original claim, the following concessions:

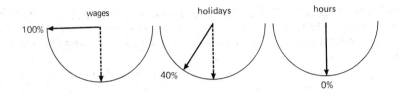

For the first time the employers conceded the wage claim in full, while the holidays were a reasonable enough breakthrough. Nothing was won on the working week; this was a blow considering the high level of unemployment at the time.

A Major Criticism

It has been said that scarcely 1 per cent benefited from the raising of minimum rates. This is technically correct, but since the wages of most workers in engineering are based on incentive payments we find that what happens is as follows:

Situation 1

Average Skilled Earnings With Incentives before August 1972 Agreement	*Minimum Earnings*	*Incentive Payment*
£30·00 per week	£19·00	£11·00

Situation 2

Average Skilled Earnings With Incentives after August 1972 Agreement	*Minimum Earnings*	*Incentive Payment*
£30·00 per week	£25·00	£5·00

The workers argued that they were putting in the same effort for far less incentive payment, so that the employers would have to 'cough up' or face trouble. In fact, since the breach had been made in Manchester, local employers knew what the offer would be at national level, so they mostly reached settlements with their own workers of across the board increases before the national agreement was signed. Thus it is probably true that fewer than 1 per cent did not benefit.

The Importance of the Manchester Sit-Ins

The workers found that the perfect answer to the lock-out was the sit-in. If the employers had got away with the lock-out, it would have demoralized the workers into returning on far less favourable grounds.

Employers were very concerned about the sit-ins and feared that they would spread. Here was a weapon used on rather a massive scale in an offensive way. This played a big part in getting the national offer increased.

A National Strike?

Some people argue that a national strike should have been called and that it would have produced a much better result. However, it must be emphasized that nearly all wage bargaining is done at factory level in the engineering industry, and much bigger increases are won in this way than through national claims. Also, the A.U.E.W., the biggest union in the C.S.E.U., has to ballot its members before a national strike can be called. The last time such a ballot was held there was an overwhelming majority against action. Indeed, the lack of response at local level outside Manchester, Sheffield and some smaller districts shows clearly that a strike would have been turned down in a ballot. There would have then been little power behind any national bargaining.

Other Tactics?

While not losing sight of the vital part played by the Manchester sit-ins in the victories that were won, it should not be forgotten that a major part of the claim, the 35-hour week, was not conceded. Could other tactics have been used which would have won this? At the meeting of European engineering employers (see Chapter 10) a British spokesman said: 'It would have been much more difficult to resist . . . a car factory on strike with all his competitors working normally.' In other words, it would have been better to pick off one important combine, such as British Leyland, and hit it, with levies from the rest of the membership. An employer faced with such tactics would find it hard not to concede the whole claim. Nor could other employers so easily expel such a big employer from their federation without harming their own solidarity.

Once the 35-hour week was conceded it would have been difficult for other employers to claim, as they did, that this could only be settled by national negotiations.

The major points to consider are:

1. Without the Manchester sit-ins much less would have been won.

2. A national strike was never on the cards.

3. Picking off one large employer would have been a better tactic.

The Post Office Strike, 1971

The Big Strike

The Union of Post Office Workers was made an offer of an 8 per cent increase in wages by the Post Office in reply to their claim for 15 per cent. They went on strike in January 1971. Seven weeks later the strike was over, with 93 per cent of the members voting in favour of the union's recommendation to return to work and allow an independent inquiry to investigate the dispute. Both sides agreed to abide by the findings.

The inquiry recommended a 9 per cent increase with a shortening of incremental scales. John Hughes, the union's nominee on the inquiry, dissented, arguing that the wage offer was far too low.

Why Call It Off?

Why did the union recommend that the strike be called off in favour of an inquiry? Why did the members agree?

Some of the major reasons were:

1. Far too many members of the Post Office Engineering Union carried out repairs in exchanges where scabs were working.

2. Private pirate postal services sprang up and workers in transport, airports and docks handled these black goods.

3. Many U.P.W. members simply carried on working.

In short, little solidarity was shown by other trade unionists.

Another important factor was cash. The U.P.W. did not pay strike money but it did give hardship payments to special cases. By the end of the strike the union's finances were in a bad way, as this balance sheet shows (see overleaf):

Income		Payments	
In hand 31.12.70	£364 400	Defence fund	£51 000
Donations 1.3.71	£203 700	Hardship payments	£1 210 450
Repayable loans	£356 000		
Total	£924 100		£1 261 450

Deficit including repayable loans: £691 350

Such hardship payments could clearly not be maintained. Why did the union not copy the miners and only pay hardship money to those who were active in the strike? This would have given many more pickets and helped stop the scabs getting into the exchanges.

Other Tactics?

The U.P.W. made this statement in their *Journal* (May 1971): 'The Executive Council believes that only by united action of the public service unions . . . can we hope to succeed.' That is one way, but it implies that alone the U.P.W. is incapable of effective action.

What about guerrilla tactics? The Post Office themselves admitted that calling out postmen one day, sorters another, collectors another, would have caused complete chaos because the public would still have used the service. (In fact, they did so in any case, even during the strike, until the postboxes were full and had to be sealed.)

What They Struck For

The gains for four typical top-grade men were as follows:

	Old Rate	Post Office Offer @ 8%	Court of Inquiry Award @ 9%	Gain from Strike
Postman	£18. 8.0.	£19.17.4.	£20. 1.0.	3s. 8d. (18½p)
Postman, higher grade	£20.16.0.	£22. 9.2.	£22.13.6.	4s. 2d. (21p)
Telephonist	£17. 8.6.	£18.18.6.	£19. 2.0.	3s. 6d. (17½p)
Telegraphist	£20. 5.0.	£21.17.0.	£22. 1.6.	4s. (20p)

The final award masked these figures because another 5 per cent was paid. This was not a wage gain but a transfer payment from an improved pension scheme which was due to come in and which the U.P.W. gave up in place of cash. For that reason the 5 per cent payment is not included above.

The Post Office worker, unlike the engineering worker, is entirely dependent on national negotiations. With the paltry sums gained as shown in the last column, who in their right mind would go on strike? It is clear that other tactics, such as guerrilla action, must be found and used.

There is one point of great importance, and that is that there is little doubt that the U.P.W. had to call off their strike. But note how independent inquiries really are when all the bargaining power has evaporated.

SOURCES

1. G. Chadwick, 'The Manchester Sit-Ins', in Michael Barratt Brown and Ken Coates (eds.), *Trade Union Register*, No. 3, Spokesman Books, 1973.
2. A.U.E.W. *Journal*, June 1972.
3. U.P.W. *Journal*, May 1971.
4. Minutes of evidence of the Hardman Inquiry into the claim of the U.P.W., 1971.
5. 'The Post Office Strike', Solidarity pamphlet.

10 The Real Face of the Employer

In this book we have seen the ball game as it is played. But is it played according to fair rules? What about public opinion and the consensus view which it is claimed that trade unionists should consider before taking action? What about the national interest?

It might appear imprudent to say that public opinion is ill-informed, yet it is true, not because people are stupid, but because employers take good care to ensure that their real intentions are kept from the public. However, in spite of the strictest secrecy, there sometimes filters through enough information to expose the real faces of the employers.

Such a case is the events of a meeting which took place just after the Manchester sit-ins in 1972.

Employers' Solidarity

According to an unofficial transcript of a meeting called by the Engineering Employers' Federation, which was attended by delegates from all the major European countries, the fourth item on the agenda was 'Employers' solidarity'.

Here are some of the points reportedly made by the delegates on the topic and what may be considered to be reasonable conclusions.

Lock-Outs

The German delegation is said to have made the point that: 'They could only broaden the front of battle by locking out the workers [who were] not striking in order to shorten the period of the strike.'

Does this sound like the voice of conciliation? Any trade unionist who made statements using words like 'battle' would be branded a dangerous subversive. There are many statements in the unofficial transcript in the same vein. It is typical of the whole outlook.

Strike-Breaking Funds

The more polite term for these funds is 'indemnity funds'. According to the transcript, all the delegates admitted that there were such funds which are raised by contributions from each member firm. Countries pay 25–90 per cent of the wage bill of a strike-bound firm. How much publicity is given to these facts? Such expenditure is certainly not mentioned when the 'need' for price increases arise. The Swedish delegate is said to have made this statement: 'There are two ways of obtaining unity: the first, as in all wars, is money.'

If the public is not aware of the class war, the employers certainly are.

Much is made of strikers getting money from public funds. How much of the contributions to employers' strike-breaking funds is classed as legitimate expenditure and therefore escapes tax?

Discipline

The employers show that they are a most disciplined group.

According to the transcript, the British delegation admitted expelling firms whose management made offers to their workers which were contrary to employer policy. The Swedish delegation admitted fining one firm half a million crowns. Contrast this with the howls of protest when unions discipline their members for acting against the interests of other workers.

Lost Business

Much is made of business lost through strikes. How then do the employers explain the rules the German employers have?

'They [other firms] may not steal the customers of a company that is strike-bound. Where new orders are placed, strike-bound firms must not suffer.'

The British are also reported as thanking their European customers for waiving penalty clauses, thus ensuring future orders during the Manchester sit-ins. These sentiments bear no relation to the claims that business and exports are lost through strikes.

Business as Usual

The transcript reveals that when the Germans announced that they were experimenting with a scheme called 'Supply Assistance', in which a firm not affected by strikes takes over the orders of one so affected, thus ensuring that contracts are met without stealing the firm's customers, the British spokesman doubted that such a scheme would work here because workers would black the work. He is quoted as continuing: 'It raises an interesting thought, though, that supply assistance might be more international than national, and perhaps this is something we should be exploring in another place at another time.'

This is most revealing and shows that though employers compete against each other, they reserve their most bitter competition for the workers.

The International Blacklist

It is well known that when workers are on strike other firms will not employ them. In fact, they are blacked, at least while the strike lasts. This has now taken on international proportions. The Swedish delegate is quoted as saying:

'We have a common Scandinavian or Nordic labour market. You can freely walk over the border. When Finland had their seven-week strike last year they asked us to direct our members in the same way as if the conflict was one in Sweden. So we directed our members, as did the Swedish Employers' Confederation, for all Swedish industry not to hire metal workers who were on strike at Finnish metal-working companies.'

And trade unions interfere with the right to work?

An Act of Conspiracy

There are two other points which show the employers' real intentions. The Swedish delegate is reported to have made this statement about employer solidarity: 'If we succeed, we can do practically anything because then we will be strong federations.'

The German delegate is quoted as remarking: 'It is particularly important to us that the association of banks and credit institutes should issue an appeal to all credit institutes that credit facilities, delayed payments, and so on, should be granted to strike-bound companies.'

Is this not a conspiracy of a band of people, small in number but strong in power, to wrestle any real rights from the people?

Who Keeps Who?

The employers need political allies, apart from organizing themselves together as some of the above quotations show. To the Tory Party and their associates who sought to lay the blame for their own incompetence at the door of the trade unions in the recent election, 316 firms donated £659 715.

This same Tory party has attempted to strangle the unions while letting the employers get away with tactics such as those shown in this chapter – a matter, no doubt, of payment for services rendered.

The Immediate Task

Public opinion, starved of the knowledge of employers' actions, cannot be a measure of how unions should fight the employers' attempts to control our destinies in the name of profit. We believe that the transcript from which extracts are quoted in this chapter is a true record of the proceedings of a meeting of European engineering employers, and if so the few facts given here should tell us that the employers care nothing for the national interest, and that patriotism is a mask behind which they hide their real intentions. Quite rightly, from their point of view, they have more in common with foreign employers than with the workers of Britain.

We are often exhorted to behave more like some less militant European trade unionists, but we have seen that their employers despise them equally, so there is no salvation in subservience.

The employers have a monopoly of capital. Against this must be set the strongest expression of working-class power we have – the trade union movement. By no means perfect, it requires democratizing, but that is our task and no one else's.

I hope that what I have said has helped some trade unionists to realize the value of the weapons and tactics we fight the employers with and has provoked others into deeper thought of new ones, so that we can all maintain that which we have won and go on to break through their monopoly of power.

Remember that we live in a so-called democracy. Without trade unionism that democracy stops at the factory gate.

SOURCES

1. Transcript of a meeting of European engineering employers in 1972.
2. 'Fact Service', Labour Research Department, March 1974.

Other books in the Trade Union Industrial Studies
series

The Activist's Handbook
Bob Houlton

So, you're an activist. But are you in control? Or is the opposition always one jump ahead?

*Can you win people's confidence? Or do they suspect your motives?

*Can you work the system? Can you keep your head when the pressure's on?

*Are you effective on committees?

*Can you handle the media? Can you put your case clearly to the press and on television?

This is a practical guide to the art of getting things done. It has been designed for active trade unionists—shop stewards, branch officials, lay delegates—and activists in all walks of life.

Bob Houlton presented the BBC TV series for shop stewards *Representing the Union* and *On Union Business*. He teaches industrial studies at Liverpool University.

Calculating

Joyce & Bill Hutton

Isn't is strange that people who can work out in their heads betting odds or the price of a round still feel at sea when it comes to more systematic calculations?

This workbook—specially geared towards practical calculations—makes mathematics easier. It deals with

*Fractions and decimals

*Ratios, percentages and interest

*Formulae and graphs

*Slide rules and calculators

This book gives trade unionists the confidence and techniques they need at work and in their daily lives.

Joyce Hutton is a former mathematics teacher who served on the Schools Council Mathematics Advisory Committee.

Bill Hutton is a former investment analyst with experience of teaching adults.

Both have had long service in the trade union movement.

Statistics for Bargainers

Karl Hedderwick

Are you losing out in the wage-price battle?

Statistics are a vital part in the complex world of
modern industrial relations. If today's trade
unionist is to bargain effectively he must match
management's statistical sources and techniques.

This introduction to statistics—specially written
to fit the needs of bargainers—covers areas such
as

*What is an average?

*How are wage rates and earnings linked?

*What is the Retail Price Index?

*How do you measure productivity?

*How to understand the unemployment figures

Karl Hedderwick is lecturer in Economics and
Industrial Studies in the Extra-Mural Department
of Sheffield University.

The Organized Worker
Tony Topham

Shop stewards are the linch-pin of trade union organization. Every day they handle a range of problems from individual grievances to negotiating new agreements.

This book is designed to help them. Based on trade union practice and experience, it describes

*How to organize a work-place and gain recognition

*How to maintain and strengthen union organization

*How to improve wages and conditions of work

*How to extend trade union controls

Tony Topham is lecturer in Industrial Studies in the Adult Education Department at Hull University.